marks, ♡ **W9-CXL-908**

DAMAGE NOTE!
3-14-11 JB/LIVN

Turner, Dorothy
    Henry VIII / Dorothy Turner ; illustrations
by Douglas Post. -- New York : Bookwright
Press, 1988.

    32 p. : ill. ; bkl 5-7. -- (Great lives)

    SUMMARY: A brief account of the life of
that complex personality, King Henry VIII of
England.
    ISBN 0-531-18203-7(lib.bdg.) : $11.90

90920   APR 89

    1. Henry VIII, King of England, 1491-1547.
2. Kings, queens, rulers, etc.   I. Title.
II. Series.

87-32569

Henry VIII

Dorothy Turner

Illustrations by Douglas Post

The Bookwright Press
New York · 1988

Great Lives

Beethoven
Louis Braille
Captain Cook
Marie Curie
Einstein
Queen Elizabeth I
Queen Elizabeth II
Francis Drake
Anne Frank
Gandhi
Henry VIII
Joan of Arc

Helen Keller
John F. Kennedy
Martin Luther King, Jr.
John Lennon
Ferdinand Magellan
Karl Marx
Mozart
Napoleon
Florence Nightingale
Elvis Presley
William Shakespeare
Mother Teresa

All the words that appear in **bold** are explained in the glossary on page 31.

First puiblished in the
United States in 1988 by
The Bookwright Press
387 Park Avenue South
New York, NY 10016

First published in 1988 by
Wayland (Publishers) Limited
61 Western Road, Hove
East Sussex BN3 1JD, England

© Copyright 1988 Wayland (Publishers) Ltd

Phototypeset by Kalligraphics, Redhill, Surrey
Printed in Italy by G. Canale & C.Sp.A., Turin

Library of Congress Cataloging-in-Publication Data

Turner, Dorothy.
   Henry VIII / by Dorothy Turner.
      p.   cm. – (Great lives)
   Bibliography: p.
   Includes index.
   Summary: A brief account of the life of that complex person King Henry VIII of England.
   ISBN 0–531–18203–7
   1. Henry VIII, King of England, 1491–1547 – Juvenile lite 2. Great Britain – Kings and rulers – Biography – Juvenile li 3. Great Britain – History – Henry VIII, 1509–1547 – Juveni literature. [1. Henry VIII, King of England, 1491–1547. 2. K: queens, rulers, etc.] I. Title. II. Title: Henry 8th. III. Series: Great lives (New York, N.Y.)
DA332.T85 1988
942.05'2'0924 – dc19
[B]
[92]

Contents

A Tudor prince

At Greenwich Palace, near London, on June 28, 1491, a son was born to King Henry VII and his wife Elizabeth. He was named Henry, after his father, and christened with the usual royal ceremony. This was the couple's third child so there were no exceptional celebrations. Prince Henry's brother Arthur, born five years before, was heir to the throne. His sister, Margaret, was only a princess and so was expected to marry a king (in fact she married the king of Scotland) but she herself was not expected to reign.

In all, Henry and Elizabeth were to have six children. Although they could not know this at the time, it was their third, Henry, who was to become one of the best remembered, most powerful and sometimes most notorious of English monarchs – Henry VIII.

Henry VII was pleased to have another son, for it made his family, the **Tudors**, more

left Henry was the second son of Henry VII and Elizabeth of York.

powerful. During the previous century England had seen bloodshed and anarchy as rival families fought for the throne. Henry VII had himself been an unimportant nobleman only ten years before, but had seized power from King Richard III. He had no great claim to the throne by birth and was afraid that rivals might take it away from him.

In order to strengthen his position Henry VII also looked for a politically important wife for Arthur, the heir to the throne. He succeeded, finding for him a princess, daughter of King Ferdinand and Queen Isabella of Spain, then one of the mightiest nations in Europe. The princess was called Catherine of Aragon. She, too, would play a memorable part in English history.

Catherine of Aragon was sixteen when she came to England.

A Spanish princess

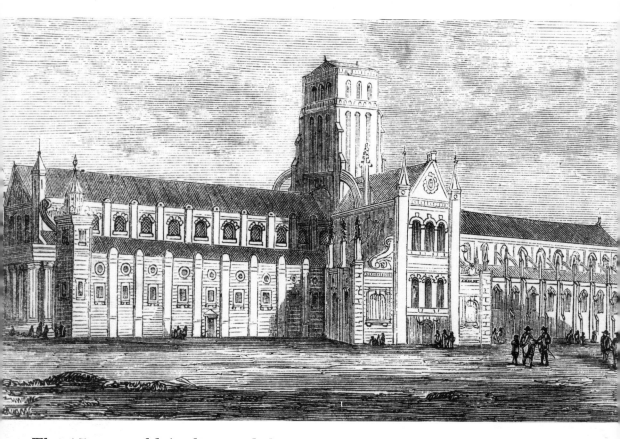

St. Paul's Cathedral, before it burned down in 1666.

The 15-year-old Arthur and the Spanish Princess Catherine were married in London as arranged in November 1501. Henry, the bridegroom's young brother, led the procession that took Catherine to St. Paul's Cathedral for the ceremony. In the many days of celebration that followed, Henry particularly enjoyed the dancing and games at court, and people commented on how lively and enthusiastic he was. Already he was smarter, more popular and more handsome than his older brother.

Arthur, supposed one day to become King Arthur and bring glory to England, was already ailing. Within five months of his marriage he had died. Now enry was heir to the throne. Catherine's parents had paid good money for her marriage and they did not want the young widow back in Spain. It was agreed that, although forbidden by the Church, Henry should inherit his brother's wife. Just before his twelfth birthday Henry and the 17-year-old Catherine were **betrothed**, promising to marry when Henry was of age.

In April 1509 the old King Henry died, and Henry VIII, then seventeen, came to the throne. Two months later he and Catherine were married and crowned with great ceremony at Westminster Abbey.

Henry and Catherine were married and crowned on June 11, 1509.

The handsome king

With the change of rulers came a complete change in style. Henry VII had been strict, self-disciplined and narrow; his son was to be the opposite.

Henry was now an outstanding figure, handsome, with auburn hair and a fit, athletic body that stood head and shoulders above most men of his time. Where his father had been austere, Henry was pleasure-seeking. He loved all sports – hunting, wrestling, archery, **jousting** and the new game of tennis.

Henry was an excellent archer often taking part in competitions and Catherine shared his interest in sport

He was also well-educated, studying **theology**, Greek, mathematics and astronomy. He was especially fond of poetry and music and became an accomplished musician and composer.

In his foreign policy, Henry's father had tried to keep the peace with his powerful European neighbors, France, Spain, the **Hapsburg Empire**, and the Pope. His son, however, had other plans. In particular Henry wanted to gain land from France. So, in 1513 he set off with an army across the Channel to Calais, which was then an English possession. For several

The battle of Flodden Field took place on September 9, 1513.

months the English and French fought, until in August, Henry won the city of Tournai.

Delighted, he returned to England to find that the Scots had invaded and been defeated in his absence. The English, under the Earl of Surrey, had marched north to the terrible battle of Flodden Field and there 10,000 Scots had been slain, including the king, James IV, himself.

Meanwhile, Catherine had borne Henry a son, but the baby died suddenly. It was the first of many such disappointments.

Thomas Wolsey

Thomas Wolsey, a cattle-dealer's son, now began his rise to become the highest power in the land. Like other ambitious but poor young men of those days, he had entered the Church at an early age. He then entered the king's service and helped to organize Henry's French campaign.

Wolsey and Henry took to each other at once, for they were both ruthless, greedy, clever and capable of cruelty. Wolsey soon became Henry's right-hand man, organizing every detail with thoroughness and energy. In effect Wolsey governed the country for Henry.

By 1514 Wolsey was Archbishop of York; by 1515 he was a Cardinal and Lord Chancellor. He amassed a huge fortune and built himself a glorious palace at Hampton Court, which rivaled the king's. He kept 1,000 servants, each wearing the Cardinal's **livery** of crimson velvet. Despite his religious vows, he became the

ather of a son. It was believed
hat he had set his sights on
ecoming Pope.

Steering a difficult course
hrough the tortuous paths of
European **diplomacy**, he
rranged peace between Henry
nd the French king, Francis I.
Henry and Francis met in
France, at a ceremony known as
he Field of the Cloth of Gold.
The occasion was utterly
xtravagant. The entire English
ourt of 5,000 people crossed the
Channel to attend. A city of tents
was erected, and huge banquets
were prepared where the food
ncluded 2,000 sheep and 7,000
onger eels. With jousting and
easting it lasted almost one
month. Within two years,
however, England and France
were again at war with each other.

Below *Henry VIII meets with
Francis I (in the foreground) at the
Field of the Cloth of Gold.*

The religious problem

Life at court was not all pleasure-seeking, nor were the king's thoughts only of glory in battle. At this time, life among the educated in Europe was dominated by intellectual unrest and ideas of reform. Philosophers, such as the Dutch **humanist** Erasmus, were visitors at Henry's court. Religion was a vital force in people's lives, but many of the clergy were unpopular. People resented paying taxes to the Church, making rich men of the likes of Wolsey, who never appeared in their parishes. The Church was also very powerful in the government of the country.

This situation was found throughout Europe. On October 31, 1517, when Henry had been on the throne for eight years, a German monk, Martin Luther, called for reforms to be made to the Catholic Church. His demands were radical: priests should give up much of their power, and be free to marry.

Martin Luther was a German monk who brought great reforms to the Catholic Church.

Other common practices Luther disapproved of were pilgrimages and the worship of saints.

Churches should be simpler, not covered in gold and ornaments, and the Bible should be the foundation of all religious teaching. In short, the **Protestant** Church was being born.

Henry was a devout Catholic. Distressed by Protestant ideas, he wrote an attack on Luther, the *Defense of the Seven Sacraments*, and dedicated it to the Pope. Pope Leo X was pleased, bestowing on Henry the title Defender of the Faith.

But the relationship between Henry and the **papacy** was soon to undergo profound strain, ending with Henry rejecting the Pope's authority altogether. Although Henry was not a radical reformer, he was to play a decisive part in the reform of religion in England.

The fall of Wolsey

One problem above all others began to obsess Henry – the need for a son to keep the Tudor family firmly on the English throne. Catherine had been pregnant many times and had given birth to four sons, but they had all died.

Only one child, Princess Mary, had survived. Catherine was forty and it seemed clear that she would not have any more children.

Wolsey receives news that Henry has stripped him of office.

To the devout Henry, only one explanation seemed possible: in marrying his brother's widow he had broken God's command. This was why God had not blessed them with a healthy son. Henry must divorce Catherine. Anyway, he had already fallen in love with a dark-eyed young woman called Anne Boleyn.

To divorce Catherine he needed

Henry's love for Anne Boleyn increased his wish for a divorce.

the consent of the Pope, (by that time Clement VII). Despite lengthy attempts by Wolsey, the Pope would not give his consent, although his refusal had more to do with politics than religion.

This was to be the end of Wolsey. His foreign policy had been unsuccessful and he was violently hated for the taxation he had forced on the people. Anne Boleyn was also determined to get rid of him. So in 1529 Henry decided his chief minister would have to go. For more than a year Wolsey lived stripped of his power and fortune. Then he was summoned to London to face charges of high treason. On the journey, however, Wolsey died at Leicester Abbey, broken and grief-stricken.

Queen Anne

By 1530 Henry VIII had ruled for twenty-one years and achieved little. His youthful good looks had gone, he was growing fat, and painful ulcers had developed on his legs. He had squandered his father's fortune. In Europe, England was of little importance.

Henry decided to replace Wolsey as Chancellor with Sir Thomas More, a lawyer and learned scholar. More was a

Henry respected Sir Thomas More and enjoyed his company. However, their friendship became strained when More refused to share Henry's misgivings about his marriage to Catherine.

Henry and Anne Boleyn. Anne was to be an unpopular queen, but she reigned for only three years.

devout Catholic and strongly disapproved of the king's plans for divorce. At first he refused the Chancellorship, but Henry angrily insisted that it was his duty to accept the honor.

Henry then called a Parliament, something that was usually done only when the monarch wanted to raise taxes. Many Members of Parliament supported his wish to reform the abuses of the Church. He got Parliament to agree that the clergy were not fully Englishmen because they owed their first allegiance to Rome, not the king. At this Sir Thomas More resigned, appalled at the way events were going.

Eventually Henry put together a **tribunal**, led by the new Archbishop of Canterbury, Cranmer, which came to the conclusion that Henry's marriage to Catherine had not been legal in the first place. So Henry and Anne were free to marry, which they did, secretly, early in 1533.

At Anne's coronation in May, crowds jeered and mocked her. Four months later she gave birth to a healthy child, Princess Elizabeth. Henry was distraught: God was still refusing him a son.

Thomas Cromwell

Sir Thomas More refused to recognize the king's marriage to Anne. So did Bishop Fisher, a holy and learned man. Despite the danger to themselves they held true to their beliefs. Henry was afraid that such powerful men could rally others around them and cause rebellion, so he ordered them both to be executed. With the death of Thomas More, England lost one of its greatest men and its finest scholar.

In his place rose Thoma Cromwell, who was to dor the rest of Henry's reign. humble parents, like Wol Cromwell had risen until he became Henry's chief m

Cromwell was eager for to break completely with so he encouraged the king further than he would hin have chosen to go. As a M of Parliament, Cromwell introduced new laws givir

monarch much more power. In 1534 the **Act of Supremacy** was passed, giving Henry total control of the Church in England. No longer was he answerable to the Pope in Rome, for was God's own representative in England. The **Act of Succession** made Anne's children legitimate heirs to the throne. Every English subject had to swear to accept these Acts.

As Henry was short of money, Cromwell found a way to provide it – by taking it from the Church.

First, small monasteries were closed and then larger ones, an closed and then larger ones, an the Church's great wealth seize Henry **leased** the Church's lan to his richest subjects, and had monastery buildings torn down

Cromwell's agents collected evidence of corruption in monasteries and used this as an excuse to seize their wealth.

A son and heir

Rebellion against the king began to break out in the north in 1536. People resented the increased prices and taxes, disliked the new powers of the king and disapproved of his divorce and the break with Rome. Each rebellion was put down, however, and more than 200 rebels executed.

Anne was condemned on May 15, and beheaded two week later.

Meanwhile, Anne Boleyn had failed to give Henry a son. Now he wanted to get rid of her, for he had fallen in love with Jane Seymour. Anne was accused of being unfaithful to Henry, was tried, and found guilty of treason Enraged, Henry had her head cut off at the Tower of London. Within a month he had married the shy, good-natured Jane. At once a new Act of Succession was

...Henry at the Royal Hunt on the morning of Anne's execution.

...assed, making Jane's children ...eirs to the throne. Both ...rincesses Mary and Elizabeth ...Henry's children by his two ...arlier marriages) were ...eclared illegitimate and sent ...way from court.

In October 1537 Jane gave ...irth to the longed-for son, Prince ...dward. Sad to say, Jane died as ...he result of childbirth. Henry ...as grief-stricken, but at last he ...ad what he wanted. He was also ...ore powerful, and richer, ...han he had ever been before.

Jane Seymour was popular, but reigned for only five months.

ays of grandeur

ry was forty-eight, growing
fatter and suffering painful
ealth that made him short-
pered and difficult. He grew
easingly self-centered and
of grand schemes.

demonstrate his importance
ad a new palace built,
such Palace, in Surrey. A
ge was demolished to make
for it, and it took hundreds of
tsmen three years to build. At
center of the courtyard stood

a huge statue of Henry. Nonsuch
Palace was a great extravagance.
Today nothing of it remains.

Around him the king gathered
a magnificent court with the
finest artists and musicians.
Hans Holbein, a German artist,
was appointed as royal painter
and his superb portraits of
notable people, including the
king, give us vivid glimpses of
the Tudor courtiers.

Archbishop Cranmer and

Cromwell were
le introducing more
it ideas into the Church.
rsion of the Bible, in
not Latin, was produced.
l also improved the
government, dividing
parate departments,
a form of civil service

Continent, however, the
g Emperor, Charles V,
Francis I of France
ice with each other after
irs of rivalry. Now they
n their attention to

destroying Protestant countries.
The Pope, too, decreed that
Henry was no longer king of
England and he called for an
attack on Henry by all Catholics.
The English, naturally, feared
invasion so defenses were built
all along the Channel coast.

*In 1536 Henry made Cromwell his
deputy as head of the Church. It
was Cromwell who ordered that
every parish should have an
English Bible and he organized
the preparation of the Great
Bible of 1539.*

Two more wives

To strengthen his shaky political position, Henry was persuaded to marry Anne of Cleves, a princess from a small German Protestant state. Henry had never seen Anne, but Cromwell described her in glowing terms and Holbein's portrait showed her to be attractive. However, when Anne arrived in England, Henry was appalled at her unsophisticated plainness. Reluctantly, he married her. Seven months later they were divorced.

Thomas Cromwell had helped arrange this farcical marriage. Now all of Henry's wrath descended on him. Cromwell was led to the Tower and, without fair trial, executed on July 18, 1540.

Cromwell persuaded Henry to marry Anne of Cleves for political reasons.

Henry married Catherine Howard privately on July 28, 1540.

n the future Henry would rule or himself, with no Wolsey or Cromwell to enrage him. Another young woman, Catherine Howard, daughter of the Duke of Norfolk, had already caught the king's eye. Henry married her on the same day that he had Cromwell executed.

The aging Henry was delighted with his lovely young bride and showered her with gifts of jewels and land. But she had other, younger, lovers, and Henry found out about them. Beside himself with rage, he had Catherine executed. For the following year he was listless and melancholy.

His mind turned back to one of his old dreams: to become ruler of France. First he would have to put down Scotland, France's ally. This his army, under the Duke of Norfolk, did at Solway Moss in November 1542. Most of the Scots nobles were taken prisoner. Devastated, King James V of Scotland died a few days later.

he final days

ry's final marriage, to
herine Parr, a widow in her
ties, was surprisingly
essful. They were married in
3. Catherine was the only one
s six wives to outlive him. As
king became increasingly ill,
took care of him; she also took
his three children, Mary
abeth and Edward, and tried
ake their lives more
able.

Henry did attempt to take France; in 1544 his army captured Boulogne, on the French coast, but it was a short-lived victory. The French king and the Emperor Charles joined together against England, surrounding Henry's army at Calais with 50,000 of their men. The English sailed home.

The wars against Scotland and France had been vastly

Catherine Parr cared for Henry throughout his illness.

e. England was very
money. To raise cash,
re increased, more
lands sold, and money
from foreign money-
Even Henry's coins were
, containing less real
silver than before.
a sad conclusion to a
reign that had started with such
energy. Henry was now unable to
walk. Depressed, bad-tempered
and frightened, the 55-year-old
king died on January 28, 1547.

*Henry died in 1547 and was
buried at Windsor. Catherine
outlived him by only a year.*

A monstrous king?

Was Henry a cruel monster, callous, ruthless and self-centered? Some people have thought so. Certainly he had those traits in his character. But we must remember that he lived in quite different times from ours. Kings then had greater personal power than today and execution was a common event throughout Europe. Other kings of his day lived more immoral lives than Henry did, and he was himself much loved by many of his subject as "bluff King Hal."

It is probable that Henry died a Catholic, but it is to him and to his reign that we owe the revolution in religion that led to the removal of many abuses and to the formation of the Church of England.

There was another side to Henry, too – the educated, accomplished musician and poet, the patron of the arts and the energetic sportsman. His was a complex personality and there are no easy answers to the question of what he was really like.

We can now see that Henry

King Henry VIII, one of England's most affectionately remembered monarchs.

need not have been worried by the problem of a male heir. Edward VI, his son, ruled for only a few years until, at the age of fifteen, he died. He was succeeded by Mary I, his half-sister. She reigned for five years, gained notoriety as "Bloody Mary" and died childless. It was Henry's third child, Queen Elizabeth I, who brought glory to the Tudors.

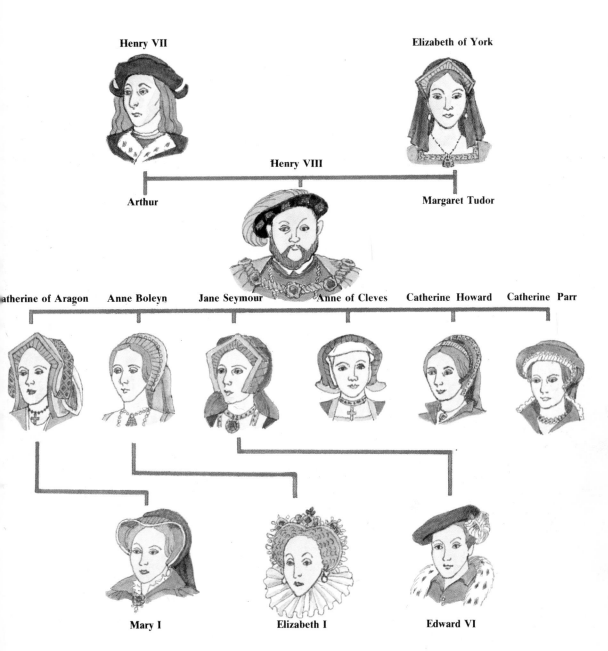

Henry VII

Elizabeth of York

Henry VIII

Arthur

Margaret Tudor

Catherine of Aragon   Anne Boleyn   Jane Seymour   Anne of Cleves   Catherine Howard   Catherine Parr

Mary I

Elizabeth I

Edward VI

'or the first time England was uled by a powerful and popular oman. Would Henry have een delighted by her success? Ie would surely have been otally astonished.

Part of the Tudor family tree. Henry VII seized the throne in 1485. Henry VIII succeeded him in 1509 and during his reign married six times. He had three children, all of whom were to rule England.

29

Important dates

1491 Henry Tudor born, son of Henry VII and Elizabeth of York.

1501 Prince Arthur, Henry's brother, marries Catherine of Aragon.

1502 Prince Arthur dies.

1509 King Henry VII dies. Henry VIII comes to the throne and marries Catherine of Aragon.

1513 English victory in France at the Battle of the Spurs. Scots defeated at Flodden Field.

1515 Thomas Wolsey becomes Lord Chancellor.

1517 Martin Luther calls for reform of the Catholic Church.

1520 Henry and Francis I of France meet at the Field of the Cloth of Gold.

1521 Pope Leo X awards Henry the title of Defender of the Faith.

1530 Wolsey dies, having fallen from favor.

1533 Henry secretly marries Anne Boleyn. Archbishop Cranmer declares this marriage to be valid. Princess Elizabeth born. Thomas Cromwell becomes Henry's chief minister.

1534 Act of Supremacy makes Henry head of Church of England. Act of Succession makes Anne's children heirs to the throne.

1535 Sir Thomas More and John Fisher, Bishop of Rochester, executed for their opposition to the king. Thomas Cromwell put in charge of church matters.

1536 Catherine of Aragon di Rebellions against Hen north of England. Anne executed. Henry marri Seymour. Act of Succes makes Jane's children the throne.

1537 Prince Edward born. Ja Seymour dies.

1540 Henry marries Anne of and divorces her. Thom Cromwell executed. He marries Catherine How

1542 Catherine Howard exec War with Scotland. Kir V of Scotland dies. Jam daughter, Mary Queen born.

1543 Henry marries Catheri

1544 Boulogne surrenders to troops.

1547 Henry VIII dies, at age Edward VI becomes kir age 10.

Glossary

Act of Succession Law passed by Parliament stating which of Henry's children were legally entitled to inherit the throne.

Act of Supremacy Law passed by Parliament by which Henry replaced the Pope as head of the Church of England.

Betrothed Engaged to be married.

Debased Reduced in quality by using cheaper metals and less precious metals.

Diplomacy The art of political negotiation between countries.

Hapsburg Empire The areas of Europe, including Spain, the Netherlands and much of Italy and Germany, ruled by the powerful Hapsburg family. The Holy Roman Emperor, Charles V, was a Hapsburg.

Humanist A scholar studying the new ideas and learning of the Renaissance – the period at the end of the Middle Ages when old, fixed medieval ideas were replaced by new ideas and the study of ancient Greek and Roman learning.

Jousting Entertainment at which knights fought each other on horseback in mock battles.

Lease To rent out land or other property for a fixed period of time.

Livery The uniform worn by all members of an important household.

Papacy The system of government the Roman Catholic Church, of which the Pope is head.

Protestant A member of one of the churches that broke away from Roman Catholic Church, protesting abuses within it.

Theology The study of God and religion.

Tribunal A group of people set up judge an important issue.

Tudors Family of Welsh origin who ruled England from 1485 to 160 The Tudor monarchs were Henr VII, Henry VIII, Edward VI, M I and Elizabeth I.

Books to read

A Child's History of England by Charles Dickens. Reproduction 1907 edition. Biblio Distributio Center.

Growing Up in Elizabethan Times b Amanda Clarke. David and Charles, 1980.

Kings and Queens of England by Dugarde Peach. Merry Thought 1968.

Queen Elizabeth I by Dorothy Turne Franklin Watts (The Bookwrigh Press), 1987.

Index